Words of Want

Words of Want

Presenting Poems and Quotes

Stephen Scialli and Friends

iUniverse, Inc.
Bloomington

Words of Want
Presenting Poems and Quotes

iUniverse books may be ordered through booksellers or by contacting:

iUniverse
1663 Liberty Drive
Bloomington, IN 47403
www.iuniverse.com
1-800-Authors (1-800-288-4677)

ISBN: 978-1-4759-6296-3 (sc)
ISBN: 978-1-4759-6298-7 (hc)
ISBN: 978-1-4759-6297-0 (ebk)

Library of Congress Control Number: 2012922420

Printed in the United States of America

iUniverse rev. date: 12/04/2012

In Loving memory of my mother and father

For DH, NS and All those I have not mentioned

"As your dreams become reality, the need for sleep becomes less as you watch the miracles happen."

Stephen Scialli

Contents

Introduction

by Darlene Hunter

"Intelligent, insightful, provocative, thought provoking and sensuous. Every now and then, you come across someone with such great talent that they stir these emotions. Stephen Scialli is one such writer. He stirs the senses and the imagination. His words are flowing, beautiful and in many cases, pure primal sensuality. He seems to have no limits as what to write about regardless of the subject matter, moods, or imagery. If Stephen writes of a touch, you feel it. If it's love, you embrace it. If it's a place or time, you see it. Even if food is the subject, you can smell and taste it. He weaves a tapestry of words, from the single stanzas, to showing the beginnings of a poem, to the finished product.

When asked if I would do the foreword for this book, I was very excited and deeply honored! "Words of Want" is an unusual title. The word "want" in this sense is used in the same manner as the word "desire". To want someone . . . desire . . . need.

I am inspired by him, moved by his words, and astounded by his talent. His style of writing is uniquely his own and he expresses it in such a way that you cannot help but feel the emotions he so expertly weaves into his work, from the tongue in cheek to the oh, so sensual. It is my great privilege and honor to know Stephen. I look forward to reading his wonderfully talented writing for many years to come."

Darlene Hunter

Preface

The poems and quotes in this book are a mix of old and new. Enjoy them as well as I have had of living and breathing them. Some may seem to be repeats, but I am sharing the progress of creation from stanza to stanza.

The poems unaccredited are all mine and poems w/ credit are those whom wrote them (of course). Thank you for reading.

Stephen Scialli

Alas, I would whisper
The words of want
into your heart
Stir the passionate fire
Make mine into your desire
Yumminess may abound
Smiles inside and out
Mood swing are found
Trying your sexiest pout
Intrigue just one
Two to be fun
Hearts racing for more
Open another of loves door
Take a healthy chance
Dive into deep water
In the lake of romance
Taught our part
W/what may ensue
Open loving heart
To feel it so true
Whisper the words
of want
into your soul

to dream the joy
of soul embrace
to hold the love
onto each other
sweet smile to last forever
no longer a chase
duly in our heart
whole in our soul
whole in our part

stephen scialli © 2012

We live in portable caves
Villages within villages
Still demanding the shaman
To cure the ills
Building walls to veil the primal wisp
Dreams burn vision
Dumbfounding the masses
Soaking blood stained misbegotten lives
Into the morass of civilization
Still demand the shaman cure our ills

stephen scialli © 2012

Deafening tone
Blank stare
Wandering alone
Persistent dare
You gave me joy
You gave me comfort
I was a happy boy
I was a good sport
The days became long
The nights became colder
My will was strong
My devotion older

stephen scialli ©2012

The words cry from my eye
Dripping venom of love
The wrong word
The right time
Spirals deep into the watery sky
Drowning soul draw
Into love heart
Beaming eloquence
Daft moves belie
The turgid move

stephen scialli ©2012

Do My words pluck
The melody
of thy heart strings
to Sweeten thee for me
Open thy heart

Play the lovers' part
a melody
Words dance upon my soul
Breathing the breathless passion

stephen scialli © 2012

Upon Thy Bed

Upon thy bed so inviting, thy body close to mine.
Thy eyes pierce deeply into my soul as thy form doth
cover me,
Thy hands infinitely strong in battle yet so gentle upon
my skin.
Upon thy bed so secluded, we lay skin to skin, as night
breezes cool us.
Thy breath is warm and sweet . . . thy lips are
commanding, and I surrender.
Two members unite in kiss and do a sensuous dance.
My body quivers at thy touch and a moist velvety
sheath awaits thy rigid sword,
To enter, to conquer, to bond; oh, to learn what doth
make my lord pleased!
Thou doest miraculous things with thy mouth; Merlin
knows no magic that compares.
Thou art wondrous and I could fairly worship thy
wondrous endowment!
Upon thy bed, I see thee in another light, in the sweet
darkening of dusk when shadow fall and heat of
passion oft rises.
I see thee in a different light when dawn doth break
and the early morning hardness of thy timber beckons
me to pleasure.

(By: Darlene Hunter ©2012)

Naked Thoughts
Fill my mind video
Luscious love
Swim deep
To my girls beach
Is almost within
My reach
I like kissing
Licking affection,
turns me on,
hot-blooded
breathing,
fingers dancing across boiling lust touch
Is that too much
As long as I am me, I shall be thee heart
As long as blood flows
As long as touch grows
We shall be parcel and part
Moist adventure
Seeking dares
Fulfill the touch
On your delicious
wares

stephen scialli © 2012

The Talented Member

Staring at my reflection in the looking glass,
I use my tongue to moisten my dry lips.
A sensual thought entered my mind,
And I marveled, "How unique is the tongue!"
So small and pink, so warm and wet,
So flexible.
Then I reflected on thy powerful, chiseled body.
Oh, how much my tongue
Would love to taste thy skin!
To use the talented member, my warm, wet tongue,
To touch and taste,
To excite and to please.
Ah, to taste thee and feel my tongue, that talented member,
Tasting and licking thy most intimate parts,
Exploring thy body, every strong, muscled inch.

(By: Darlene Hunter ©2012)

Vibrant hues
Cover the blue

Twinkle, twinkle

In the sky

Adorn
Enjoyed
In my eye

stephen scialli © 2012

hard water stains
on the soul
Scrub a life away
as
no amount
of prayers
can open
the broken window
of dreams

stephen scialli © 2012

The Love Letter

My darling, let me try to tell you how I feel. If my heart were made of words, it would be easy to tell you how I feel. I'd have all the right phrases, all the right inflection, so that there would never be a doubt, as to what I meant or tried to say so clumsily at the moment.

I'd have the right amount of words and not go too far in expressing what I feel deep inside.

If my eyes could speak what my heart feels, you'd see more love than you've ever seen before.

When the emotion of love is expressed, sometimes I cry . . . not in sadness my love, but because the love is so overwhelming.

If my body was a great work of literature, you need only to look at the words there and know that the union we share is worth all the words that could ever be written.

My love, my dearest, look at me. See the end of a journey that you've taken to find real love, And the beginning of new walk with someone who will never leave your side—a new journey, a new adventure, a deeper friendship than you've ever known, a love that keeps you warm, secure, happy, content, and more loved than ever.

Hold on, feel my heart in these words. Touch my face, my lips, my body-feel the physical expression of an inward love.

Touch my heart again with your words, the looks you give me, and the touch of your heart to mine . . . feel the deep, abiding love that bonds us together as one.

I am one with you and you with me . . . always. Be with me, come to me, and let me come to you . . . to give each other the love we've both searched for and longed for . . . for so long.

From the depths of my heart, with every fiber of my being . . . I love you.

(By: Darlene Hunter ©2012)

Good night sweet dream

Light a candle
Your smile
lights my world
Light a candle
Slip your shoes off
Light a candle
Massage your feet
Light a candle
Effleurage your calves
Light a candle
Massage your thighs
Light a candle
Peel away the day
Light a candle
Glory at the pearly gate
                    of heaven
Light a candle
Smile as your rosebud winks
Light a candle
Run through your landing strip
Light a candle
Joy of softness
Light a candle
Look into your eyes
Light your candle

stephen scialli ©2012

Without You I Break

Without you, I break.
Each day passes slowly . . . time has no meaning
Your voice, your presence is rarely heard or felt.
My heart longs for the nearness of you . . . the warmth
of you.
Tears flow like torrential rain . . . the hurt is like a swollen
river of pain.
Hope is but a glimmer . . . some distant faint glow.
Seemingly unreachable in the deepest abyss,
Looking up I cry out . . . and you don't hear me.
Without you, I break.

(By: Darlene Hunter ©2012)

Lost in the beauty of your eyes
dreamily swimming
your velvet pool
sweet wet joy begins

stephen scialli ©2012

Two Souls

Doest two souls dare reach out for affection?
To be lost in the maze of emotions that make up love?
My heart feels so much for thee.
My mind is sometimes consumed with thoughts of thee.
It feels as if my body aches for thy touch, thy kiss.
To feel thy hands so strong, commanding my every move,
And thy mouth demanding and thou doest feel my surrender.
The white columns open to thee, surrounding thee,
Giving in to the basest of desires,
Raised hips receive completely thy swollen virility.
The mounds of flesh with hardened tips press into thy massive chest.
They ache for thy lips to taste, to kiss, to suckle.
The breaths we breathe are raspy and ragged.
Two souls combine to become one in the most intimate of unions.
Oh, the sweet pleasure of succumbing to each other!
Mirrored pleasure of two bodies prepares to fan the deep fires
And the longing for release begins to burn deeply within our bellies.
The journey our bodies have but taken is culminated to this;
The cries of passion reaching the ultimate climax of lust, of desire, of love.

(By: Darlene Hunter ©2012)

I Dream of You

I dream of you . . . though you know nothing of my dreams.
My heart is touched by your words, moved by your intensity
And I tremble at the thought of you.
I dream of your face so close to mine that I feel the warmth of your skin.
I dream of your mouth nearing mine and with the barest of touches,
I melt into you.
Dreaming of you touching me, looking into my eyes
Is the sweetest of things.
I dream of your voice . . . is it deep?
Is your voice soft? I dream of hearing it . . .
I dream of feeling your warm breath on my ear
As you whisper to me.
I dream of you . . . I hope for you.

(By: Darlene Hunter ©2012)

"the feelings, the best words are never recognized until it's too late to enjoy the real reason"
May 5th, © 2012

stephen scialli © 2012

Lost words
drift away
in the catacombs
of our dreams

stephen scialli © 2012

Deep Desire

O love of my heart, thou dost make me shiver with desire.
Thy touch sends a glow as white-hot embers to the very
core of my womanhood,
Silky, smooth wetness is the product of thy touch and
thy kiss.
Thy body strong and lean; thy hardness increases and
presses against me.
Oh, sweet love of my dreams!
If thou wouldst take my words, have them come to life,
words of love, of lust and desire,
My heart would soar, my flesh would burn and my body
wouldst be thine.
Touch me here amid my field of dewy moistness; touch
the soft flesh of my breasts.
Thy sword of passion plunges into the velvet portion of
my womanly heat.
Thy lips a source of bliss, to bask in; an intensity I have
never known.
Over and over, we are immersed into the waves of
incredible desire
And the very beat of our hearts seem to be in like-cadence
with each other.
Thy hands so rough in combat, yet they so gently caress
and linger on my body.
Thy eyes blaze with a different light-the light of desire,
lust and need.
Battle cries replaced with cries of wild, intimate abandon,
reaching the ultimate peak.

(By: Darlene Hunter © 2012)

caressing the floor
sun dancing beam
arrives
the new day
shining
new dream
in
our
glorious
way
heart swells
to gleam
your reach
in my grasp
Sun dancing beam
harkens the way
hearts new glean

stephen scialli ©2012

Your passion fills me w/joy
Your words are the filling
Yummy digestion
Eternal bliss found
Under the quarter moon
Filling the void
Of no loss

Prove it always
Shred the doubt
To tiny confetti
Shower onto the false floor
Falling into oblivion
never to seek doubts
Again
Ever

dreamy delights surprise
the leather tiger
the kitten purrs in his grip
deep driving passion
swells his animal
growling
clawing
purring
it's a beautiful day

stephen scialli © 2012

"The saddest part of human existence is self imposed loneliness."

stephen scialli ©2012

your soul is beautiful
crying for love
i feel your soul
reaching the heavens
Bringing smiles
for those that love you
like me

stephen scialli © 2012

feel the heat
feel the passion
feel my breath
feel my eyes
feel my voice
feel my words
feel to heal
taste my love

to be lost
in your arms
I would die
each night
darkness gone
to be passion
to be alive
to die each night
feeling your smile

stephen scialli © 2012

you do not need firewood for your stories . . . you do not need it rains in August . . . six emotion in the emotion, the emotion because you are . . . patches do not try to mend clothes crumpled, because you are not a patch . . . love is a painter, not a character, although sometimes these Two things seem to fit . . . you are a director, not an actress of your life . . . Unlike the characters in novels who need applause of their audience to draw their existence, why do not you exist . . . you create, you know, stay in front, beside and behind better than a shadow, because you are true . . . art is pure harmony, and you also: the beauty of your soul so you paints . . .

By Deni D

In the valley

of womanhood
a wonderland wanting
yes, wanting to be
explored
devoured
enveloped with lips on lips
skin to skin
so velvety smooth
is his touch
breathing her name
hearing her sighs
the soft sighs
of a woman . . . .

By Wanda Christienson ©2012

Your moist flower
Greets me w/dew
Engulfing me
Enter the velvet envelope
Feel the impending deliciousness
Surrender the new dawn
For the now

It is not a new wow
From time immemorial
It's the same
Nothing new
No blind tutorial
Yummy primal stew
It begins
Slow froth grows
Slow movement
Feel it free
Sweet surrender
Soul sings to me

Gripping joy
Milks

To feel your soul
Cry out to me
smiles inside and out
Joy to be free

Secret dream
In your head
Nothing
you have said
Your soul scream
To release
Let me help
If you please

stephen scialli © 2012

Willow never had a song. This was an attempt to address that. It takes place after Tara's murder, transitioning into the events of Two To Go and Grave . . . . Ms Heather Petrites wrote:

speak to me in riddles,
girl, I'll never know the truth
the pain inside my soul's so hard to bear
what once we'd found we since have lost
an ironic twist of fate

a promise is . . . a promise is . . .

a promise is a . . . . lie

i've found solace in the silence of a dark night
and if you ask me how i feel
i'll say "i'm alright, baby"
saccharine sweet deceptions fall from my lips

shattered in the face of fear,
you're slipping away
embraced by guilt, i cry, negotiate
Isis hears me . . . . and turns away . . .

inside my heart has folded, a decrepit hand of cards
but long live the queen (am i unseen?)
said long live the queen (i am unseen)

around i go . . . around i go . . .

around i go tonight

i've found solace in the silence of the darkness
yet if you ask me how i feel
i'll say "sleep tight now, love"
but my empty heart's fallen all to pieces
said my heart's been torn down now to
pieces

oh Diana, my goddess. Hecate, please?
Please, help me.
Osiris, are you out there?
Horus, heed my call
Save me from myself . . .
Save me from myself . . .
now, you've gone, the Emptiness,
it eats me up inside
the haunting shadows of the past
drift quiet past the door
She follows me, tormenting me,
I cannot hide this time
Each choice I made, slip closer to the grave
engulfed in smoke and fog . . .

it's so hard to live without you by my side
the pain just radiates within me
flowing though my veins
(novocain)
no matter how i try . . .
i cannot live this lie . . .

what can i say to undo what has been done

to undo the hurt that has been done

tell me I'll find solace in the silence of the dark night
don't ask me how i fell because
i lost you, dear heart
my soul's gone black
my resolve's cracked

i've nothing left to lose . . .
said i've nothing left to lose . . . .
speak to me in riddles,
girl, I'll never know the truth

the pain inside my soul's so hard to bear
what once we'd found we since have lost
an ironic twist of fate

a promise is . . . a promise is . . .
a promise is a . . . . lie
i've found solace in the silence of a dark night
and if you ask me how i feel
i'll say "i'm alright, baby"
saccharine sweet deceptions fall from my lips
shattered in the face of fear,
you're slipping away
embraced by guilt, i cry, negotiate
Isis hears me . . . . and turns away . . .
inside my heart has folded, a decrepit hand of cards

but long live the queen (am i unseen?)
said long live the queen (i am unseen)

around i go . . . around i go . . .

around i go tonight

i've found solace in the silence of the darkness
yet if you ask me how i feel
i'll say "sleep tight now, love"
but my empty heart's fallen all to pieces
said my heart's been torn down now to
pieces

oh Diana, my goddess. Hecate, please?
Please, help me.
Osiris, are you out there?
Horus, heed my call
Save me from myself . . .
Save me from myself . . .

now, you've gone, the Emptiness,
it eats me up inside
the haunting shadows of the past
drift quiet past the door
She follows me, tormenting me,
I cannot hide this time

Each choice I made, slip closer to the grave

engulfed in smoke and fog . . .

it's so hard to live without you by my side
the pain just radiates within me
flowing though my veins
(novocain)
no matter how i try . . .
i cannot live this lie . . .

what can i say to undo what has been done

to undo the hurt that has been done

tell me I'll find solace in the silence of the dark night
don't ask me how i fell because
i lost you, dear heart
my soul's gone black
my resolve's cracked

i've nothing left to lose . . .

said i've nothing left to lose . . . .

Heather Petrites © 2012

like a mouse in a hypnologic maze
wander 'round—Liberace haze
silent screams; don't say a word
can't look forward . . . or haven't you heard?

feel the cold touch on the back of my neck
stinking breath—my heart's a wreck
so why do I miss it so?
come on baby, there ain't no where else to go . . . .

i wonder why
i wonder why
i remember
aftershave

dried blood under my nails
wonder what else this entails
happiness—a moment, an instant—
too late . . . i know this isn't it

so do i live to tell the tale?
a brief story—a siren's wail?
Pocahontas waiting all alone
seal it darlin'—no one will ever phone

i wonder why
i wonder why
aftershave
i remember
your aftershave

Heather Petrites © 2012

Under his mane
He is quite insane
Dead plastic flowers
Floating past
Spiral rivers
Drowning scream
Cloudy dream
Nothing last
Forever past
Needed
    Cloudburst of joy
      on the stream
of sorrow

stephen scialli © 2012

The day is not dreary
But alas I am weary
My love is afar
She is a bright, so bright
Shining star

stephen scialli © 2012

Your hazel eyes
Shed lies
Around my heart
To feel warmth
All over
In every part
Desirable delight

stephen scialli © 2012

Slip and slide into the emotional need
Feel the smile of your moist adventure
Greedily exchange moist moments
Delightfully dive again and again
Red shoe dance fit for a new goddess

stephen scialli © 2012

I was driving down the road and saw ALL the neon glory . . . brightly lit lies hence:

Hollow words ring out in my eye

Cherished love seen in my ear
My mind an empty vortex
No longer fed on fear

Multicolored Madison Ave
Blinding true sight
Lost in a world
Flooded by avarice avenues
Day and night

Heading out on the road
The endless night

stephen scialli © 2012

Since my baby left me
I have no where to go
Stuck here in Philly
Listening to the radio

stephen scialli © 2009

The night is the mystery
Which you never see
Out in the dark
Your mind wanders free

May be the heady draught
Or it may be naught
Imagination running free
Soon you shall see

stephen scialli © 2012

Opening a green Door
Delivering a dream
Fiery cool stream
Your eyes cry more

Petition of sins isn't waged away at the dark door
Sins attrition must be washed away many times

Darkness behind the door
Greeting the fervent admission
Dimming admonished blind ears
Blooms man doom of fear

stephen scialli ©2012

Beats of the heart
flushed face
we will not part
just to have you
near me
touch me
feel me
the desire of you
in my heart
makes life always new
your embrace I feel
butterflies fluttering
in my stomach's space.
Satisfied

stephen scialli ©2012

breath to my soul
dream of your embrace
the true hold
my heart beats
primal desire
fueled
by the angel
of love
my soul breaths
you

stephen scialli ©2011

gods I want to see a smile
on those luscious lips
traveling a moist adventure
while electric tremors
travel erotic tracks
to my station
deep within
your moist motor

stephen scialli ©2011

My soul speaks
Not some scant feeling
Violet blue love
Blooming
Driving
deep within
The well of souls

stephen scialli ©2011

Desirable delight
drinks the time
to drown troubles
No treat denied
No Never said
Filling dreams
Drenched sweet
Fiery Flame rises
Blinding Boredom
Drawing forth
Mondo Miracle

stephen scialli ©2011

"Brooke"

Not just a breed
of any kind;
tall,
powerful,
yet blonde and fair.
Short-haired,
it contrasted her;
long haired,
it made her shine.

She, with long hair
blonde,
body petite
quite beautiful.
Eyes deep,

sensuous
gleaming,
made my time
    stand
       still.
Protected
by her guard dog,
wrapped up
    at night,
       safe.

Me,
her shining knight,
yet I know,
now she is the better!

Carmine Coronato, Jr. © 2012

you make my soul smile
Dancing chakra
Swim through the clouds
To feel your being

you give me flight,
no matter the distance
I am there w/you
Chakras singing
Living the past
In the now

smiles abound
thoughts
return for more
day may end not
w/o memories
Of you
Sweet friend

stephen scialli ©2012

Such passion, just hold me tight
and talk all night to me
I shall be lovely free
Soon my sweet beauty of the
night
Secret dream
In your head
Nothing
you have said
Your soul scream
To release

Let me help
If you please
You fill my soul w/elation
Simple flight to another joy
No land nor sea can keep me
No chains on my heart
As long as you are in my life
Any part

Dawn is the essence of you
brightening the world when she
smiles
bringing joy to living creatures

everywhere
as you do
to this blue tiger

I believe we are luminescent
beings
Chakras matching wits
Distance never a hindrance
For two in tune w/each others
omance

I feel your brain dance
To taste the tingle
Beloved warm chance
Smooth velvet wrinkle
Kisses to wake your soul
Kisses to warm your toes
Kisses to feel your heart
Kisses to remove the pain
Kisses until you enjoy
The gentle rain
I feel your brain dance
To taste the tingle
Beloved warm chance
Smooth velvet wrinkle

stephen scialli © 2012

I think sex
I think breath
I think sweet
I think sweat
I think dreamy death

stephen scialli © 2012

Your passion fills me w/joy
Your words are the filling
Yummy digestion
Eternal bliss found
Under the quarter moon
Filling the void
Of no loss

stephen scialli © 2012

"Real Power in life is to negotiate w/pain
Till it is a memory of annoyance"

stephen scialli © 2012

Alone I wait for the dark mistress
No one around no one to hear
The sorrow of the dark tomorrow
Nothing in it to really fear
Stranger is the joy of birth
Surrounded by laughter and mirth
Followed by hollow joy of strangers
Is it a boy or a girl
Bully for the boy in this world
Loneliness descends
I await the greeting
Of the dark mistress
Firm is her hold
Forever left cold

stephen scialli © 2012

we kiss
to never part
we touch
to make us start
we feel
to make us smile
no matter apart
the distance of the miles
drives our loving heart
to never be alone
if we are apart

stephen scialli ©2012

looking
into the deepest blue
dancing delight
of electric flight
i see the joy
deepest in you
every single time
every single night
eyes of which
i would
forever adore
dancing electric delights
of the deepest blue
hidden behind
your heavenly door

stephen scialli ©2011

I wait my love . . .
while my breath erratic
My heart rapid
My chakras
delightfully dancing
My steel nerve strong
The drum beat in my ear
drowning all thoughts
Dream of desire
running through my head
Weak resolve on an ancient promise
Your arms swallow me
Hearts rhythm bounce us
to
nirvana

stephen scialli ©2011

dream wonderful
to live the joy
on the soul
bring the delight
to the surface
do not hide
do not run
run w/me
to the dawns
burning desire

stephen scialli ©2011

your eyes burn desire
your heart is set a fire
I am free in your arms
as they hold me tight
you are passion charm
in our delicious night
we long to hold
we long to be bold
in loves haven
we misbehaving
I want to live
forever in your heart
once we fill
our amorous part

stephen scialli ©2011

deep within we find
a deeper well
a source of infinite
love
we keep a lid
to protect ourselves
on top
it needs to be free
open
to be fresh
for you
for me
for the world
to see

stephen scialli ©2011

The long road to thee is barren and cold . . . but the warmth of thy heart bids me not surrender.
Thy arms of strength hold mine course and sweet words beckon my soul . . .
The distance may be great and the journey harsh and long . . .
Yet no distance is too great that thy love cannot make more bearable
The only surrender in my mind is the one of giving myself to thee
and the sweetest moments that awaits our souls to touch and unite.

By: Darlene Hunter © 2011

I don't want your eyes
I want them to adore me
as I adore You w/mine
I don't want your body
I want your soul
to be In Love
w/mine as my soul
is In Love
w/your soul
I want you to Live and Love
next to me not just from a distance
I don't want your lips
I want the feeling
they give to me
and mine to you
I don't want your touch
unless your embrace is ours
to feel forever given freely
I don't want your heart
unless it feels the joy as
my heart does
I want to share
your heartache
your pain
your joy

stephen scialli ©2011

I reach for you
deep in a dream
I am lost
till I feel true
your touch
my skin smiles
me heart soars
too much
just a dream

stephen scialli ©2011

w/that beautiful face
full of joyous grace
a smile
from heavenly place
draws me to you
beckons me
for my soul
to be yours
never to be dark
to taste love
to fly
through the heaven
a free bird
never be caged
always loved
by you
in this world
my tigress
my girl

stephen scialli ©2011

no one ever said you couldn't be In Love
w/more than one. no one ever said
it couldn't be done
it is a desired plan
by many in this world
to have to have their cake and their girl too
or boy in your case
I want your happiness to be true
as your best friend I will always come through
I don't know if you ever read my words
this just makes me sad
so blue. but alas I am your friend
to the very end
nothing can change this ever
so live to the best
I will never abandon you
I am here till the very end
Always for my so very special friend

stephen scialli ©2011

tree branch reaches
to the sun for love and life
w/leaves for more life
my branch reaches for you
to create new leaves
each day to love you
needed cloudburst of joy
on the stream of sorrow
your soul shines the seed of love
to grow into your poem
into the tree of smiles
To breath life
into darkness
to smile
unto my world
to bring
your burning bush
great delights
when my branch douses
w/delicious might

stephen scialli ©2011

I would like to sit w/you
To Listen of your day
I would like to sit w/ you
Massaging your neck
I would like to sit w/you
As you relax
I would like to sit w/you
Just to be close w/you
I would like to sit w/you
To ask you how you feel
I would like to sit w/you
To have you feel
I would like to sit w/you
To let our hearts hold each other
I would like to sit w/you just to feel your heat
I would like to sit w/you
So my soul can feed your soul how to love again
I would just like to sit w/you
I would like to sit w/you till time immortal
I would like to sit w/you hands holding fingers entwined
I would like to sit w/you to share each others air and strength
I would like to sit w/you because you are you
I would like to sit w/you staring at the stars
I would like to sit w/you to share the scene
I would like to sit w/you is our dream

stephen scialli ©2011

I need a taste of your lips
to dream of your swaying hips
I need a taste of your love
to send my soul soaring above
I need a touch of your heart
so our souls never part

stephen scialli ©2011

forever each moment
to live in the dwelling
of the soul
to hold each other
to feel hearts melt
into one
quakes tremble shake
each moment we make
to chase pain away
to love everyday
in a myriad
of delicious ways

stephen scialli ©2011

Not in this lifetime could I express
The utter joy of knowing thee
Sweet knight of my heart
The joy of thy words . . . the magic of thy touch.
Oh, sweet surrender of body and soul!
If I could but touch you . . . even once-
Though only once would never be enough;
To touch thee not, would be a far greater sin . . .

By: Darlene Hunter © 2011

look at me at days end
all the aches, pains
fade into mist
when I feel your smile
draws up strength
to love you
to hold you tight
w/all my might
all the hardship
just a vanishing trip
on carousel of life
to scream out loud
I am another fallen cloud

stephen scialli ©2011

Thinking of your eyes
looking up at me
as you glide
as you hummy
as you yummy
as you make smiles
as I bite my lip
as you warm me
oh so yummy
like chocolate
in my tummy
your turn
now
as I look up
to enjoy yummy
to circle the button
to feel the love
to taste the joy
you give to this
one happy
one smiling
one satisfied
jersey boy

stephen scialli ©2011

I am in lustful love
w/you
I am desire molten fire
w/you
I am spectacularly alive
w/you
I am lusciously In Love
w/you
I am joyfully desired
w/you
I am alive
w/you
I am the Tiger
w/you
You are my Tigress
so true

stephen scialli ©2011

I am very oral
like to lick
like to tease
like to smile
like to please
oral is my
favorite style

stephen scialli ©2011

Thou hast brought to the surface
The sweet nectar
In which I wish thee to drink . . .
And to taste thee
And for thou to fill the deepest part
Of my most cherished gift . . .
My heart . . .

By: Darlene Hunter © 2011

touch yourself
be feeling
to dream
reality sweet
drive the joy
to the surface
leave the lies
behind
drink
of
my
hearts
eye

stephen scialli ©2011

I always try
to take time out
to write
sometimes when I write
food burns
sometimes not
the word
is important
not to say the food is not
but unlike food
if the word
is not told
it is far worse, than
food getting old

stephen scialli ©2011

I would love so much
to have your touch
each and every day
so our love
would hold sway
to tickle your fancy
to create new smiles
to love and dance
all sorts of styles
to sleep each night
in the arms
of my love
to share
each others charms
Lust, Living, Life
w/joyous delight

stephen scialli ©2011

Lust, Living, Life
my pen strives
to complimentary write
the joys and sorrows
of creatures we meet
on the crazy street
called life
the ups and downs
are full of fun
if you're scared
life will have you
on the run
so I face each day
walking that street
looking for my love
looking for fun
each step a joy
each breath fresh
each new friend I meet
each old friend I greet
make me happy
make me sad
one thing for sure
I am always glad
for friends
that endure

stephen scialli ©2011

Cumulative theory
Can be so dreary
Cumulative cure
Always sure
I want you around
No matter what you do
Even when I feel down
I want you true
It's 100 degree
When I look into the cloud
Your face appears
from above
To show me
My true love

stephen scialli ©2011

Falling cloud
fill the emptiness
you left behind
Hiding the dry tear
in the sky
The beauty
in my being blind
Draws Picasso portrait
in the minds eye
Drawing on a happy illusion
Doesn't change the conclusion
Makes me Sad, sad, sad
Makes me Mad, mad, mad
The sky of a fallen cloud
brings ephemeral silent joy
To this naughty bad boy

stephen scialli ©2011

she seeks one of finance
I am the passion
I am the Lover
I am the Romance
I am not soulless pleasure
but a golden treasure

stephen scialli ©2011

my soul swells w/passion
dream of desired lover
fills the emptiness
between our embrace
thoughts of breathless passion
bring special smile to my face

stephen scialli ©2011

this man of wit and taste
can be in your arms post haste
The call of my heart
is already a part
of your soul
Yes this heart of gold
one day you will wrap
your willing arms
to enjoy my witty loving
charm

stephen scialli ©2011

waiting for my Lady
sundown comes and goes
the seasons transpire
Waiting for my Lady
dawn comes and goes
the seasons inspire
waiting for my Lady
moon shrinks and grows
the season desires

stephen scialli ©2011

most deliciously
this bad boy
writes poetry
hungers for your touch
can reveal all so much
can not sit still
strong my will
to kiss
to tell
our story
the glory

stephen scialli ©2011

black hand owns my soul
not bought w/black gold
love no more all done
it is at the end of my one
she once held it warm safe
it holds my heart bare unprotected
it squeezes when I try to feel
layers and layers begin to peel
love shrivels at her touch
all I've done so much
meaningless the past
it brings sorrow and tears
all the unwanted fears

stephen scialli ©2011

time for you

Time is crested
Along creation joys
fueled by one love
Drowning in a lake sorrow
Saved by thoughts
to bring life/love to the
living beach
maybe in the morrow
it will be within
reach

stephen scialli ©2011

passionate love
mere words are not enough
Distance precludes the inevitable
Soul swimming in unison
Eyes lovingly gaze
velvet smooth skin
held close
against leathery
battle scarred body
Joys not withheld
Unabashed loving
Breeds beauty, of
Electric Butterflies,dance
all along your field
Jolts of smiles
appear on your lips
time and time again

stephen scialli ©2011

my heart beats rapidly
through my chest
my breath escapes my lips
past the lump in my throat
to feel the warmth
to feel beauty
your soul shines
to me

stephen scialli ©2011

looking into your baby blues
Time stands still
My breath feels alive
Electric jumping beans
course through me
Butterflies bounce
in my brain
just looking into your
beautiful baby blues

stephen scialli ©2011

I want to kiss
every inch
of you,
your legs,
your arms,
your rosebud,
your derriere,
your soul

stephen scialli ©2011

lullaby

time for bed to sleep
I fall to slumber
w/you in my mind
tall in lumber
thought
of you divine
cuddle tight
close to me
Hold me right
Put out the light
kiss of sweet night
sleep to dream
my serene
dreamy queen

stephen scialli ©2011

my marilyn

you are my Marilyn
I am your Frost
you thrill the world
you are more
you are greater
than you know
you are life

stephen scialli ©2011

i am a mess

i am a mess, the kind of mess you dream about when you
are alone
i am a mess, the one you think about when you are w/
another
i am a mess, that makes electric rain falling all over
you
i am a mess, the one that loves you and you love so much
it hurts
i am a mess, but I am yours body, soul, and full of loving
kisses that are yours alone

stephen scialli ©2011

Lacey

for you
to be quivering
w/thoughts
of blissful trembles
running through your field
over thy mountains
of fertility
to those very beautiful eyes
as they stare
at me
lovingly
lustfully
delightfully
hold me forever
in heart
as well
as body

stephen scialli ©2011

only wearing smiles
desires driving daisies
long forbidden miles
of loving crazy
your field fertile plain
whispering the fire
right on a precipice
now a heavenly choir
joy across your lips
makes a day worthy
bouncing delicious hips
makes happy boy from Jersey

stephen scialli ©2011

a delicious woman,
she holds me true
unless lies spring forth
to turn me blue
til the time immortal
my heart will be true
til I am dust
my thoughts are of you

stephen scialli ©2011

Yummy petals
deliciously fondled
lusciously licked
to open
to explore
to moisten
to sup
on heavenly
nectar
is true joy
for this
bad boy

stephen scialli ©2011

sweetest garden of thy womanhood,joys yet to be known! soon all will revel on our desires being brought before the gods! thy bed shall be all the nature before us, thy creek, thy field, thy mountains, thy valleys and all that is before us! my creme shall be filling thee as thou shall make thee a ring of joy around mine face,lips succor thy flavor!

sweet dream faire maiden thee, until our lips meet, we shall suffer the tortures of the damned, once met all heaven shall open up for you and me

stephen scialli ©2011

our beauty
is not just your breast
tits sag from time to time
your legs are so gorgeous
beauty to heaven
which is mine
Your eyes tell the world
of my beautiful girl
so smart so sexy so fine
I like all your parts
the one I like best
is your heart
I once had a hole
in my soul
it is full and alive
now w/you by my side

stephen scialli ©2011

a poem
to share w/you I wrote

You are so kind and sweet,
but take care,
I am not to be trusted,
in a flash
your knickers would be by your feet
now that would make your day
and mine
sweet
Complete

stephen scialli ©2011

I can not sleep
while my heart doth weep
all is gone from my world
the one I love this girl
hath crushed my heart
it once had been hardened
for years it was cold
she had a key that opened
the part
it was dark and old
she brought a light
to my life
all was gone
no strife
now that part is again
closed
the door shut tight
while my heart is weeping
I can not sleep this night
dream well all children sleeping
all is not lost
price was paid a high cost
do not be discouraged
do not lose hope
this heart belongs
to the biggest dope
w/a noose around his neck
made of hardened heart rope

stephen scialli ©2011

September 11, © 2011

Nothing can break the American Spirit!
We stand United or we will fall apart
Our Freedom is our importance
deep down in The American Heart
it makes us strong to stand
United w/each Hand In Hand
Creates the greatest Country
In The world
for all the American Boys
for all the American Girls
Bring Our Troops back home
now shout out to them all
"You do not stand alone!"
Let the world know our might
Let the world know
We sleep safely each night
because Our American Girls
because Our American Boys
Make it safe around the world
Now shout out to them all
"You are not alone!"
bring our American Boys
bring our American Girls
back safe to their home

stephen scialli ©2011
this

September 11, 2011

not a moment goes by
w/o my thoughts filled of you
you spread your legs before me
lips winking so true
call out my name to come
return to me forever
I am not done
your smooth velvet skin
beckons attention
fill me w/enchanted dream
again and again
I have not passed you by
it all started by you saying "hi"
feel the time slip away
loving freedom this day
lost in the arms of my beloved
to reach a place we all covet
at peace within ourselves

stephen scialli ©2011

fireworks of my dream
spill forth into the world
carrying love
for my beautiful girl
nothing stops the burn
nothing stops the passion
all the creative joy
for you from this one bad boy
so light up my sky
drive away the darkness
passion lights up
your beauty in my eye
far beyond the mundane
to sparkle my soul
w/your beauty untold
passionate your flame

stephen scialli ©2011

I can not make you love me
I can only show you I care
show my beating heart
it has no need, no repair
gone are the prayers
gone all the despair
filled w/loving desire
hungry for your care
long as I make you smile
my day is complete
no matter the distance or miles
I can feel your heart beat

stephen scialli ©2011

tongue time
spread 'em
dessert is mine
lapping
lapping
delicious
honey
wine
bolts
of joy
warming
warmer
EXPLODE
electric rain
senses
drain
delightful
life
live
full
w/you
sweet baby T
you
are
the one
for
me

stephen scialli ©2011

your fiery passion
your desired eyes
drive men wild
gorgeous thighs
I own your soul
you own mine
where they dance
eternal time
where wild ideas bloom
to grow true passion
deliciously deliriously bold
from two loving souls

stephen scialli ©2011

home and bone weary
I rest my head on your breast
to feel your beat of your heart
just running my fingers glide
inside your hot velvet slide
beating faster you part
legs so beautiful
a moan a shudder
you deliver
my weary bones
my head rest
on your beating breast

stephen scialli ©2011

I can't buy you houses
I can't buy you cars
what I can give you
is the sun
the moon
the stars
The Love for you is great
The Love for you never held
The Love for you never late
The Love for you Always felt
Not a price on our love
Not a price on your soul
freely I give you mine
not for any gold

stephen scialli ©2011

you are the creation of joy
the brief eternal happiness
not some silly play toy
for others that may be
some sexual congress
not for me alone
our love is deeper
than the ocean
my love your keeper
no mater the time and space
my soul has found it's place
not for any reason
just for loves permanent season

stephen scialli ©2011

nothing could be neater
divine spooning
warm form delight
could ever be sweeter
after a long hard night
desires never run cold
when love runs deep
sweet arms do hold
even in your sleep
when first you stir
sun hits your face
deliciousness incurs
kissing all parts
especially your
beautiful face
this starts our day
wickedly sweet
wonderful way
greet the world
w/you
my beautiful girl

stephen scialli ©2011

your eyes of beautiful blue
make me want to feast
on you
in such a lovely way
to turn me into
a sexy beast
so true
your soul gleams
twinkle of our eyes
match all of the heavens star
to make such a beautiful dream
to cherish our hold
to caress our souls
make loving bold
until forever told
all is in your hands
hard as gold
I spend in you
a diamond you do hold

stephen scialli ©2011

it was at the moment
deep within her
5 places I was touching
3 no one could see
her heart
her soul
her brain
deep in her
darker place
piston playing there
my thumb running along her mouth
she sucks it in as she screams out
she loves it in the back play
sweet one
deep eyes cries
Any given day

stephen scialli ©2011

poems
I
Love to write them
w/my huge romantic heart
need another start
to seal it up right
cold ripped part
needs warm
gentle healing
from the love cart
so suit up to have fun
warm the moist motor
make this boy happy
seal his heart
w/warm moist part

stephen scialli ©2011

thinking of your eyes
looking up at me
as you glide
as you hummy
as you yummy
as you make smiles
as I bite my lip
as you warm me
oh so yummy
like chocolate
in my tummy
your turn
now
as I look up
to enjoy yummy
to circle the button
to feel the love
to taste the joy
you give to this
one happy
one smiling
one satisfied
jersey boy

stephen scialli ©2011

I am awake
w/throbbing love
ready to make
you quake

thoughts drift to you
laid bare before me
open inviting true
beautiful sight to see

a delicious woman,
she holds me true
unless lies spring forth
to turn me blue

till the time immortal
my heart will be true
till I am dust
my thoughts are of you

stephen scialli ©2011

I always try
to take time out
to write
sometimes when I write
food burns
sometimes not
the word
is important
not to say the food is not
but unlike food
if the word
is not told
it is far worse, than
food getting old

stephen scialli ©2011

I am in lustful love
w/you
I am desire molten fire
w/you
I am spectacularly alive
w/you
I am lusciously In Love
w/you
I am joyfully desired
w/you
I am alive
w/you
I am the Tiger
w/you
You are my Tigress
so true

stephen scialli ©2011

sadness stems
from being alone
not true
w/this boy
every place
is home
every eye a lie
not true
w/this boy
truth is the joy
blue as the sky

stephen scialli ©2011

I am very oral
like to lick
like to tease
like to smile
like to please
oral is my
favorite style

stephen scialli ©2011

tempting taste
electric rain
tingling toes
to
favorite follicles
bringing smiles
curling your toes
bringing
more
electric rain
keeps
falling

stephen scialli ©2011

road to my heaven
paved w/good intention
all along your thighs
leaving butterfly kisses
upon all
the soft seductive nest
to slurp honey nectar
to have you bite
your lip
smiling
while
I am away

stephen scialli ©2011

w/o you
words
are
stuck
in
the
deep
muck
    and
      mire
never to swim
never to surface
to
be
known
w/o you
words

are stuck
deep
muck and mire
never to swim
never
to
surface

never
known
to spread
the joy
w/o you
words are stuck deep
in
muck and mire
never to swim
never to surface
never known
to spread
the joy

©2011 stephen scialli

beautiful sunrise
the golden dawn
greeting moist eyes
w/devoted kingdom
draws nigh
the soft parade
leading
golden rays
encompass
wrapped
warmth
inside
the
living
blanket

My Calendar

sinfully scrumptious Sunday
moaning magical Monday
tempting tasty Tuesday
wickedly wonderful Wednesday
terribly terrific Thursday
freaky fun-time Friday
satisfyingly sexy Saturday

©2011 stephen scialli

each day we strive
for the little death
serenity
piece of nirvana
in the arms
of my love
to enjoy
immortality
for
the
brief
moment

©2011 stephen scialli

my heart leaps
at the beauty of dawn
The cool air breathes
new life
Shining bright my angel
brings green love
New fresh diamonds
glitter from dusty sidewalks
Silver lined clouds fall earthward
Howling Moon kisses goodbye
Horizon smiles
Opens her arms
consumes me
Back to dust
Back to nothing
To return again to nothing
To return to forever
But one heart I have
it gives much love
My one heart beats only
for one
Belongs only
to
one
Love

©2011 stephen scialli

sadness
overwhelms me
empty bed weeps
the covers barren
remembrance
sweaty bliss
haunts the sheets
dew of you
still lingers
in the air
your scent
still fresh
in
my
minds
eye

stephen scialli ©2011

friends
never
have
to feel sorry
in life
w/friends
to let them be who they are
to allow you to live life
not to be anything but,
best friend
lover
companion
sexy
magnificent woman
you are to me
so never
feel sorry, just kiss me
feel sad, hug me
feel horny, show me
feel adventure, let's go

stephen scialli ©2011

building, building
until the dam
weakens
resolve
a feeling
FULLNESS
BURSTING
electric joy
flows
freely
to
drive
peace
down
your
lane

stephen scialli ©2011

yes,
I am
something
else
to hold
to love
to caress
to lust
to love

do what you must
do what you think
no matter what
my soul does drink
my love to you
the love is yours
through time immortal
through all the swinging doors

stephen scialli ©2011

I'm sitting here all by myself
just trying to think of something to do
trying to think of something,
anything just to keep me
from thinking of you
But you know it's not working out
because you're all that's on my mind
One thought
is all it takes
to leave
the rest
of the world
behind

stephen scialli ©2011

I can't make you do anything
You don't want
I can't make you feel
If you don't want
I can make your soul sing
If you give me a chance
I can make you feel
If you want sweet romance
I can't tell you with who
you want to be
I can only show true
The love I have for you
You need to meet
some other creature
In some lonely place

Driven by mad desire
At a distance
I am at a loss
Only up close
Can I help stem your fire
It is true
I am madly in love W/you
My soul belongs to no other
But you crave lust
Too
So do what you must
It may make my heart blue
Always remember
I will always be In Love w/you

stephen scialli ©2011

I look up in the skies
I look carefully
> *to see your face*

I am lost in the lovely place
I wonder if you're there
I wonder how you fair
I wonder if you think of me
I wonder if you'll let me tell you
That looking at the stars
makes me think of you
no matter how near or far
looking into the skies
to see the stars
I want to be lost
in your eyes
to hold you tight
forever and ever
all through the night
for you to know
to never let you go
stephen scialli 2011

Your soul is imbued
W/my love for you
It knows I care
It knows this true
The way my soul grew
Feeling in love w/you
To Trust in your heart
They will never part
It is not what I take
It is what I give
Mildly do not make
Not to ever forsake
No claim have I
On your body blue
Where it may be
Just true I am
Madly in love w/you
Do as you must
Forever not long
Totally I trust
The decision
Where you belong
In my arms
Holding you tight
On any warm
Or cold night

stephen scialli ©2011

I would rather be dead
than miss out
on a redhead
being alive is a crime
to miss
such beauty and grace
to miss
I would be out
of my head
to pass up
to skip by
a gorgeous red
so now
understand
you are now
my new plan
no matter your hair
I like all of you
so fair

stephen scialli ©2011

Love's Dilemma

Biggest problem in love
Good guy gets wrong girl . . .
Good girl gets wrong guy . . .
They fall in love
Good ones get cheated . . .
Now the good guy thinks
all girls are fraud . . .
Good girl thinks
all guys are flirt . . .
When good guy
meets
good girl
they avoid falling in love
become
just
good
friends . . .

stephen scialli ©2011

dream dancing
tantalizing temptress
envelopes everything
daring delights
fortunate feelings
guide goodness
arrow around
dive delights
dream desire
dancing demure

stephen scialli ©2011

dancing delight
delicious delirium
draws decision
down definite
dew demand

stephen scialli ©2011

I want your heart
to share,
to feel
to sigh w/joy
to get wings
to know love
again

stephen scialli ©2011

"Money can't buy what we give to each other. Love and time are precious commodities. No one has power, we give sway to those we love. We all are hurt at one time or another by each other, the ones that are worth it are worth any suffering."

Stephen Scialli ©2011

"Fear is an illusion we place on ourselves which hinder our lives~!"

Stephen Scialli ©2011

flash of Eden
revealed in your eyes
daring me to chance
daring me to dance
my sense
so sharp
I feel your eyes
dancing the rumba
to the beat
of our hearts
forever
  and
      ever

stephen scialli ©2010

dawn breaks
everlasting joy
courses through me
your body awakens
to my touch
eyes closed
your smile widens
at my exploration
sweet fiery electric
is better
than
any bitter coffee

stephen scialli ©2010

words are music to the soul
wordless speech escapes her lips
immaculate dream weaves soul drama
lost in a vision of creation

stephen scialli ©2009

you are my muse . . .
words pour forth
from my fingertips
when I think of you
naked alive
in my mind
in my heart
owner of my soul

stephen scialli ©2009

your soul cries out to me
destined desire w/o the mire
liquid love flows from vein
to nurture lustful fire
chakras dance
primitive lance
velvet love
velvet kiss
liquid love

stephen scialli ©2009

grace moves
across the ground
not seeming
to touch
the earth
dressed
   in
      diaphanous
            beauty
              exposed
to all glory
touches
run
electric
to shrieks
      of
        bliss
cries
      of
        joy

stephen scialli ©2009

so sexy . . .
so romantic . . .
send our souls
to the moon
for the eternal
second
delicious embrace
sup on your fruit
as you ripen
to advantage
flowing honey wine
drips off
my chin . . .
as trembles
become quakes
of bliss
so slippery
so wet
movements
become hurried
seeing the golden dawn
appear to engulf
us
both

stephen scialli ©2009

you repose on the sheets in the beautiful light
sly smile placed upon my face
striking innocence exudes sexy respite
lure of the animal draws me to your grace
not enough to be so far away
the treasure of my soul laid out on lace
draws my love to you this day time and place

stephen scialli ©2009

silent speech makes music for the soul
silence escapes her lips
immaculate dream weaves soul drama
lost in a vision of creation

stephen scialli ©2009

your undulating hips signal
the spark of breathless renewal
soul binding joy rippled
through your meadow
forming a grin of delicious sin
on your lips
breathless passion anew
triggers signs
of spring dew forming
in your fertile pasture
marking moist heaven
awaits
my tending

stephen scialli ©2009

you are the essence of the dream
a given desire of an angel
swept into mankind's grasp
to enlighten our souls
w/kindness of sexual beauty
driving men mad w/feverish passion
you weave a tapestry of love
to consume all evil and hate
in the path of your coming

stephen scialli ©2009

deep within your eyes our embrace is stirring
no lies can hide the eternal reward
your eyes care your lips dare
naked your legs spread before me
your soul laid out to bare
anxious apprehension fills the emptiness
alone is a thought lost
lonely an expensive forgotten cost

stephen scialli ©2009

I love so much
I love so hard
while I can
I deny no one
whose soul
is pure
so why am I
alone

stephen scialli ©2009

Julia

my beautiful Julia
my heart is throbbing
my throat is dry
my dreams are wet
delicious
delightful
are
full
of
YOU!

stephen scialli ©2009

My Wild Love

my wild love
has found me
my wild love
has kissed me
my wild love
has held me
my wild love
is forever
my wild love
is leaving
my wild love
is gone
MY WILD LOVE
IS NO MORE
MY WILD LOVE
IS GONE

2008 stephen scialli

"The beautiful things in Life are worthy of keeping close to your heart and to share them with all who touch you."

stephen scialli ©2008

the winds of fate
shall be driven
w/compass of desire
to point to true love

2009 stephen scialli

the winds of fate
shall be driven
w/compass of desire
to point to true love
w/animal passion
guiding through
the darkest
of waters
to find you
again in my arms

stephen scialli ©2009

the scents of old
belongs somewhere
wafting away
daydream array
subtle and real
my mind it feels
the scents of the young
time not lost
swaying away
another daydream day

stephen scialli ©2009

we lay in our bed
passion flame
linger in my head
desire dance
across your velvet
          ballroom floor
w/no loving shame
only the gaze
of loves
          wide open door
we lay in our bed
passion confession
run through our head
no shame no dread
by what happened
next in our bed
loving lingering
moment of fun
never ever
to be outdone

stephen scialli ©2009

sing the body
sing the many
sing the blissful
sing the release
dance on fire
dance on electric fire
dance across fertile fields
sing the joyous
sing the release
sing for the eternal second
sing
sing
sing
sing the passions note
sing, sing, sing
as yesterday
is no more trouble
sing the new found relief
sing, sing, sing

stephen scialli ©2009

when our lips meet
you will only think of me
when our hearts touch
you will only desire me
when our souls sing
we will have each other
forever

stephen scialli ©2009

yes, let me into your world,
yes let me into your soul
yes, let me into your loin
yes, let me into the love
yes, let me into the fire
yes, let me into spoils
yes, let me die in your arms

stephen scialli ©2009

I woke up in dreaming of a passionate embrace
I woke up in tumescent desire of blue
I woke up lost in your velvet place
I awoke alone w/fiery delight of you

stephen scialli ©2009

I woke up in dreaming of a passionate place
I woke up in tumescent desire for you
I woke up lost in your velvet trace
I awoke alone w/fiery delight for you
I woke up in dreaming of a passionate embrace
I woke up in tumescent desire of blue
I woke up lost in your velvet place
I awoke alone w/fiery delight of you

stephen scialli ©2009

kisses
to make you forget
the pain
the anguish . . .
licks
to make you swoon
w/delicious delight
embrace
to lose ourselves
for even the briefest
of moments is respite

stephen scialli ©2009

I dream of us
velvet kiss
of velvet goodness
drips honey
from your lips
honey drips
from my lips
down my chin
armour of illusion
falls away
showing me
the truth
enlightenment
O' bringer of joy
O' bringer of passion
waves of passion ecstasy
undulating fiery electric
creating epiphany of reason
only if love were so simple
a reason
to enjoy
through
and
through
in all life seasons

stephen scialli ©2009

Day In Day Out

each time i think of you
my breath has stopped
day in day out
my breath comes back
each day i hold my breath
afraid the garlic i love will
chase you away
day in day out
i never know if you even see
the way i breathe
when you are near
day in day out
you shape the way i live
the air i breathe
day in day out
when i die
remember
day in day out
my last breath
was yours

stephen scialli©2008/2004

Your Eyes

Oasis
in your eyes
flowing waterfall of love
to an Island
in your heart
to the country
of your soul
make words
of poetry
flow
from
my heart
my soul

stephen scialli ©2008

love

The road to love
is filled w/beauty
and heartache
worth every pang
to feel your joy

stephen scialli ©2008

Newly Born

Each day
I am born
anew
refreshed
w/you
in
   my
     life

stephen scialli ©2008

What Do You Think of?

what do you think of?
with our bodies
naked
locked
exploring
what do you think of?
the laundry
the food
the car
what do you think of?
the groping
the clasping
the sweating
what do you think of?
what do I think of?
I think of you
how glorious
the brief moment
of pleasure
w/you
to stop
the pain
before
we
are
dust

stephen scialli ©2008

I want you . . .

I feel a tugging
my inner being
swept up in you
I want you
so bad
I want you
for you
I want you
it's driving
me mad
I want you
my blood
burns
I want you
so bad
driving me mad
I want you
My passion
inflames
I want you
holding tight
my arms
tremble
I want you
to see into
my being

stephen scialli ©2008

ocean of space

between us
an ocean
of time
and space
it only
binds
us
stronger
I sail
through
the ports
willing
believing
In our love
Circe
could not
stop us
as the Gods
      gave their blessing
Love as ours
  knows no bounds
Love as ours
  is infinite
Love as ours
  fills the world
w/life

stephen scialli ©2008

fool as I

am I a fool
to love someone
so much
am I a fool
to care
am I a fool
to love so hard
am I a fool
of course
I am the fool
my heart once
light and full
is now

hard
heavy
empty
w/sorrow
tears
fill my eyes
as my
heart breaks
in tiny pieces
for a fool
such
as
I

stephen scialli ©2008

I Am Free

I am free
my heart
is chained
to one
as it will
always
be
never to love
another
but free
to roam
the earth
never
to love
another
one

stephen scialli ©2008

One as Us

Beware the strength
that love holds
on one as us
Beware the barriers
fallen before
on one as us
Beware the worlds
Beauty shown
on one as us
Beware the lovers
embraced form
on one as us
Beware the time
endless to begin
on one as us

stephen scialli ©2007

A Look

Your picture always wants me to touch you
to run my fingers through your hair
to feel your breath on my chest
your lips on my lips
to look into your eyes
love to love
to feel ALL of YOU
not just one part
but all of you
I am very in touch with your soul
as you are with mine
you make my soul sing
a melody of love
sonnets of soul song

stephen scialli ©2007

Lost Time . . .

No matter
how we choose time
time chooses no one
as we embrace
it runs faster
but it does not
it
is
we
who
are
lost
in time
ourselves

stephen scialli © 2007

Soul Ministry

our eyes locked
in the secret labyrinth
of the soul
key we seek
to unlock
the dreams
wandering in your eyes
my fingers dance
across smooth valleys
treeless mounds
bare caves
into the garden
of earthly delights
your taste is on my lips
your dew is on my skin
as thighs lock
sends waves
through me
through you
A Sigh
A CRY
A whisper of devotion
we may never

loose our touch
The dream hardens
songs are sung blue
swaying
to the wild breeze
Bliss of Mystery
release
of the primitive
breathe a sigh
of comfort
sweat glistens
across you
the dew
of morning love
sent washing
over us
I wish all
could
feel
my sweet love
in the ministry
of
love

stephen scialli © 2007

tongue dances

We run to each other
in clothes we are born
looking
into each others eyes
Fingers
dancing
in each other
running w/creamy goodness
raise to our lips
we
taste
Eden's
Forbidden Fruits
Smile crosses our lips
they meet
to allow
dances w/tongues

stephen scialli © 2007

feeling of joy

I miss the touch
   of lovers
      feeling of joy
I see
   my minds eye
   drawing pictures
   of my lust
   in
   your
      embrace
sweaty
delicious
      embrace
I awoke
     bold
THROBBING w/desire
As
dreams
become
reality
w/you

stephen scialli ©2007

I Count

I count the moments
I count my breaths
I count my heartbeats
I count my miles
I count the kisses
to allow me
to count my blessings
on meeting you

stephen scialli ©2007

A Moment

as each moment
we melt into being one
feeling each fiber
our souls
burning with lustful love
never being quenched
but satisfied
we kiss
for
all
eternity

stephen scialli ©2007

the eternal cure

I'd like to feel
an eternal second
the eternal moment
where
we
are
one
mingling as two
into
one
running
stream
of Ecstasy
caressing our souls
we two bags
of humanity
shedding ourselves
to confront love
in all our glory
to revel
in loves
delicious stew
sensitive

we
have
become
to each thrust
new waves
bring pleasure
each movement
new waves
as
we
ride
the waves
crescendos
the shore
our bodies
ache
when we are apart
only each
others
touch
cures

stephen scialli ©2007

When

when do we love
is it your eyes
that drives my desire
when do we love
is it your touch
that makes me burn
like fire
when do we love
is it your walk
on angels clouds
not devils mire
when do we love
whispers in my ear
flaming heat
into swollen pride
when do we love
the first dawn

of each
new days light
brings my heart
to you
when do we love
in each nights
vision of lustful fire
when do we love
with the intake
of every breath
passion is our desire
when do we love
every eternal second
we know
of each
other
beating heart

stephen scialli ©2007

My First Poem

The Boardwalk

I awoke with the sounds of gulls
cawing away
stretching cat like
to feel supple
relaxed
for all my 13 summers of my life
full of optimism
raging w/hormones
seeking the mysteries of feelings
today was the simplest of pleasures
thumbing to the boardwalk

stephen scialli

This was written when I was 13, budding poet was coming into his own!

Preview

And the poems just keep on coming! Stephen's unique style shows up once again in his next project called ***poem for you***. Striving to keep the insatiable appetite for his work at an uphill pace, these next poems are just as brilliant as his earlier published works. The poems seem to speak to the individual. The passion and fire seem to pierce the soul. Keep watching for updates for the next release. For now, please enjoy these few selections from the heart and essence of poet Stephen Scialli.

poem for you
I feel your smile
to my soul . . .
it burns as ecstasy . . .
.warms the depths
of my being
2008 stephen scialli

poem for you
My heart still tugs,
when we talk,
makes the world
seem smaller,
when love speaks
through the heart.
2008 stephen scialli

*poem for you
each day brings
new light to ourselves,
new breath to our bodies,
new sight to our souls,
new love to our hearts,
new understanding of our pains
2008 stephen scialli

*poem for you
swirling leaf
gentle breeze
soft kiss
the thought
of a soft touch
inspire me
2008 stephen scialli

*poem for you
our being
is enough
each holds
half the puzzle
2008 stephen scialli

Look Stephen's fan pages on Facebook.
https://www.facebook.com/pages/Words-of-
Want/217067895090692

https://www.facebook.com/
WindInMyHead?ref=ts&fref=ts

Also email at the addresses below:

windinmyhead2012@gmail.com

wordsofwant2012@gmail.com

Interview with Stephen Scialli

About the author

October 2012

When compiling this bio, it was decided to do it as an interview. Therefore, it is my great pleasure to introduce Stephen Scialli.

Interviewer Rita Green: I am really honored to be interviewing you, Stephen. I am a great fan of your work. Tell me, where do you hail from originally?

Stephen: I was born in Tokyo, but I grew up in what I call a non-English speaking area known as New Jersey. *smiles*

Rita: Care to expound on the Non-English speaking area comment?

Stephen: A place called Lanoka Harbor, Lacy Township. Yes, they speak "Americanese". *more smiles*

Rita: (laughing) Now, that is an interesting way to describe where you lived. You make your home in another state now, right?

Stephen: Yes, I live in the Great State of Texas, a place called Seminole. Of course, like in Lanoka Harbor, there are no real Seminole natives anymore. Lanoka means "Lucky Indian" in Lenape. Not a single Lenape within 200 miles of my old hometown!

Rita: Concerning your poetry, what inspires you?

Stephen: Women. All of them. (Sly smile) Life throws a muse at me all the time, if you read the signs. Could be anything, but ultimately, "beauty shared is beauty enjoyed."

Rita: That answer is inspiring in itself. Do you have a set form or routine you follow when you write? Or, do the words just flow?

Stephen: They flow from my fingertips, sometimes with a life of their own.

Rita: For those of us with curious minds, would you tell us a few of your favorite things to do when you are not writing?

Stephen: Women. (Mischievous smile) Ok . . . I like to ride my Harley, travel to places, eat good foods. Read when I have time, cooking is a passion too. Love to ski . . . Anything to do with water . . . boating, fishing, skiing and jet ski. I'm a surfer too.

Rita: Wow! You have such a variety of things you enjoy. Sounds like a full life! If you could say one thing to aspiring writers to encourage them, what would that be?

Stephen: Write what you feel, not what others say you should write! Whether it be horror, fiction, sci-fi, bios . . . go with your heart. Poems have no right or wrong in my way of thinking.

Rita: That is great advice. Now, Stephen, could you give us a few words about your new book of poetry called "Words of Want"?

Stephen: It's a bit of passion self help for those who need some guidance.

Rita: Very well put! I'm sure there are other works of yours to be seen in the future?

Stephen: Yes, I have so much to write and have written so much. The future is full of new passions to enjoy. Those are past and never again, to today and future we begin.

Rita: Thank you, Stephen, for your candid answers and your charming wit.

Stephen: My pleasure to be interviewed by a lovely lady such as yourself.

Rita: Thank you again, Stephen, that was very sweet of you. I look forward to perhaps interviewing you again sometime.

Stephen: As do I.

Cover photograph by:
Stephen Scialli
with iPhone 4
2012